The Golf Insider
Performance Diary

The Club Edition

Contents

The Club Edition
The Golf Insider Performance Diary

Welcome to the club edition of the golf insider performance diary. This book will help you achieve your golfing dreams.

You are about to embark on a 21-week course of practice, play and education to improve your golf.

Every two weeks, I will introduce something new to develop your golf practice routine.

After each lesson, please carry forward the useful practice games and drills. Each lesson gives you a new building block to add to your golf practice schedule.

Over the 21 weeks I hope to give you a great insight into how to monitor your play, effectively practice and help transfer your performance onto the golf course.

By the time you complete this performance diary, you will have a full tool kit of games and ideas to help you improve your golf.

This performance plan takes the work I do with golf professionals and provides it in a format you can carry round in your golf bag.

Every two weeks there will be a short lesson and explanation of what to do. To add to this, I have included QR codes and links to key readings and videos of skills games.

If you're new to QR codes, just open up the camera on your phone now and hover it over the square below. It should automatically read the code and take you to the webpage online. If this doesn't work for you, I have also included the web address.

On that fine note, here is your first piece of learning – Three ways to practice to improve your golf. This article is the perfect place to begin your journey.

http://golfinsideruk.com/golf-practice-3-ways-practice-golf/

The following pages give you an introduction to the structure of the book and how to record your progress.

How to use this book

I truly believe there is no limit to how good you can become at golf. The first step is to examine how you currently play golf – number of putts, chips and direction of shots off the tee and into the green are all golden nuggets of information. Once you have this information, you need to create high-quality, specific practices to improve the areas limiting your performance.

Your golf practice should be divided into two areas:

1. Practice that refines your technique.

2. Practice that develops your golfing skill.

If you're serious about performing I also suggest fitting in pressure practice at key times during the season.

Every week your practice schedule should be refined to optimise your rate of learning and golfing performance.

Keeping track of this can be tricky, so I decided to design this diary for you. Each week you have three pages to complete:

1. Playing stats

2. Technical practice

3. Skills games practice

There is also a fourth page every week for notes. Please use this as you choose. I wanted to provide some flexibility for all those who I hope this diary will help.

On the next few pages I will explain how to get the most out of completing this performance diary.

Playing stats

Turn to a *playing stats* page and briefly scan it. The idea is for you to fill out this page each time you play, either after your game or during. It should take less than five minutes.

I won't need to explain the top section. This is a swift overview of your score, up and downs, putts etc.

Below this section we have a mock fairway and green. This allows you to add directional detail to your long game performance.

Replay each hole in your head and mark an 'x' where your tee shot finished, then mark an 'x' where your approach shot finished. Once you have completed all 18 holes, you should have a clear picture of you long game performance.

Golfers don't like reflecting these stats when they play badly, but this information is golden for informing your practice.

Weekly practice: technique

Nearly all golfers take part in technical practice. However, I find few golfers practice as efficiently as they could do. Rather, they are *going through the motions* on the golf range. Filling in the weekly technique page aims to optimise your rate of change and progression.

First of all, set clear aims. Alongside your aims you should have a more detailed swing thought or feeling. Your aims and swing thought can both be recorded in the sections on the top half of the page.

The next two sections are where most golfers fall down. If you make the correct swing, what ball flight should be produced? And if you don't, what shot(s) will occur?

In tandem with shot outcome, you need to identify the triggers for good and bad swings. That is why I've included a feedback section. I'd like you to answer how you *know* you've made a good swing. It might be a towel under your arm, your divot pattern, or videoing your swing. My key point is this – learning does not occur in the absence of feedback.

To finish your session, I suggest you tally up your number of reps (balls/putts hit), a rough estimate of how many good swings you've made, and some points to take forward to next weeks practice and play.

Weekly practice: skills games

The aim of golf is to get the ball to your target, or as close as possible. Unfortunately, few golfers spend time focusing on this aspect.

Each week I suggest you dedicate time to improving your level of *golfing skill*, alongside your technique practice.

These skills games should be focused on the areas you need to improve. Check out your playing stats. Do you need to hole more putts, reduce hooks off the tee, or improve your up and downs?

I will have a growing database of skills games on golfinsideruk.com. However, if you are ever stuck for ideas, send me a message and I will do my best to help you.

Each skills game should have progressions to make it more difficult. I've left a little space for you to note how you have set up your skills games each week. Once you're done playing your skills games, write down your scores and how much time you invested – this could be the time it took, or the number of balls you hit.

I've left space for three games per week. For a club golfer this is a good aim if you wish to improve. However, if you complete more – great! Just use the weekly notes page to add in extras.

Before you set off on your golfing quest

To become great at golf, you need to invest time into highly effortful, specific practices. This includes time spent playing golf, working on technique and completing skills games.

This book doesn't replace that process. It ensures you keep a track of the stats that truly matter when it comes to improving your golf.

Goal setting is a great way to keep you on track. To help, I've added two extra sections: 'hours to awesomeness' and 'top scores'.

On the next page you have *hours to awesomeness*. I suggest each month you set yourself a target of how many high quality hours you wish to invest into your golf game.

At the end of each month, work out if you're ahead or behind of your target. You can also check how much time you invested in each area.

The *top scores* section is as simple as it sounds. Keep track of your top *skills game scores*, each time you beat your top score for a game; update this section. I've left these pages open for you to create your own design.

Keep a note of your favourite skills games, each time you beat your highest score, come and update your progress.

Have great fun on your golfing quest.

Hours to awesomeness:

Month	Technical practice	Skills games	Play	Total	Target
Jan	12	8	12	32	30 (+2)
Grand Total					

Top skills games scores:

Top skills games scores:

Week 1: Hugo's range challenge

Let us begin the process of improving your golf. It's week one, so we're going to start by putting a key block of practice into your schedule – long game skills games.

Skills games are a critical, yet under utilized, type of practice by many golfers. This week you're going to play Hugo's range challenge, for a more detailed read, follow the QR code below.

http://golfinsideruk.com/golf-practice-games-long-game/

If you're just ready to get going, follow the instructions below:

Head to the range/practice ground with 40 balls. Create one of the following target zones at 200 yards (this can be a rough guess).

- — Easy: 20 yards wide
- — Medium: 15 yards wide
- — Hard: 10 yards
- — Pro: 5 yards wide

Begin with your Sand Wedge. Your aim is to hit a shot that lands within the width of your target zone. Don't worry about the distance of your shot, as long as it lands within the *target width*.

If you miss, try again with the same club. Once you succeed, move down to your next shortest club, a Pitching Wedge.

Your aim is to work your way through your golf bag, with the aim of landing each club in the gap before you move onto the next club - 9, 8, 7 Iron... all the way through to your Driver.

Your 'score' is what club you get down to with your 40 balls. If you run out of balls and you've made it to your 7 Iron, '7 Iron' is your score.

Feel free to start on the easy level. This game can feel like a breeze until you get down to your longer irons!

Best of luck and enjoy!

Let me know how you get on with a pic @golfinsideruk on Twitter and Instagram.

Weekly playing stats

Score to par: ___   Net score: ___

Eagles: ___   Up & downs: ___/___
Birdies: ___
Pars: ___   Sand saves: ___/___
Bogeys: ___
DB+:   ___   Putts: ___

F.I.R.:   /

L Trouble	L Rough	Fairway	R Rough	R Trouble

G.I.R.:   / 18

Key area(s) to improve:

_____

_____

Weekly practice: technique

Practice aims:

1. _____

2. _____

Technical thoughts:

Desired change in ball flight:

Key pieces of feedback:

Summary

Number of reps completed: _____

Percentage of good swings: _____

Areas to improve in practice:

_____

_____

_____

Weekly practice: skills games

Skill game 1: *Hugo's range challenge*

Set up & notes: *15 yards wide*

Difficulty: *Medium*

Score: *4 Iron*

Time/reps completed: *40 balls*

Skill game 2:

Set up & notes:

Difficulty:

Score:

Time/reps completed:

Skill game 3:

Set up & notes:

Difficulty:

Score:

Time/reps completed:

Weekly notes:

Weekly playing stats

Score to par: ___   Net score: ___

Eagles: ___   Up & downs: ___/___
Birdies: ___
Pars: ___   Sand saves: ___/___
Bogeys: ___
DB+:   ___   Putts: ___

F.I.R.:   /

L Trouble	L Rough	Fairway	R Rough	R Trouble

G.I.R.:   / 18

Key area(s) to improve:

_____

_____

Weekly practice: technique

Practice aims:

1. _____

2. _____

Technical thoughts:

Desired change in ball flight:

Key pieces of feedback:

Summary

Number of reps completed: _____

Percentage of good swings: _____

Areas to improve in practice:

_____

_____

_____

Weekly practice: skills games

Skill game 1: *Hugo's range challenge*

Set up & notes:

Difficulty:

Score:

Time/reps completed:

_____

Skill game 2:

Set up & notes:

Difficulty:

Score:

Time/reps completed:

_____

Skill game 3:

Set up & notes:

Difficulty:

Score:

Time/reps completed:

Weekly notes:

Week 3: Putting basics

Okay, hopefully you've succeeded in a few range practices with Hugo's range challenge. I'm also hoping that by now you have collected a couple of playing stats. Playing stats are key for noting weaknesses and understanding how to shape your practice to best improve your golf.

Another critical skill for improving your golf is solid putting. It can be tricky for club players to make time for putting, so I have a challenge for you. I want you to create a 5-10 minute putting drill you can play at home or before you play on the putting green.

The aim of this putting drill is simple – check your alignment and get focused on starting your putts on line.

The QR code on the next page can be used to see my own version of this game (it is seriously tough). For you to start building your very own game here are my key steps.

Take a few balls and find a straight putt on the putting green. At home you can use a small glass jar as a target.

Easy/Medium: One putters length.
Hard: Two putter lengths.

You have 20 attempts to see how many putts you can hole. Your score should be how many successful attempts you had out of the 20.

If you want to check your alignment, lay a club down next to your golf ball, ensure the club shaft points to the right edge of the hole/target. Then lay a second club parallel along your feet.

This is a crude, but useful way to check your alignment and swing path.

This game should take 5-10 minutes, but forms a critical piece of lowering your scores. Once you achieve 20 out of 20 on your chosen distance, move back to make it more challenging.

http://golfinsideruk.com/how-to-become-great-at-putting-with-one-drill/

Weekly playing stats

Score to par: ___   Net score: ___

Eagles: ___   Up & downs: ___/___
Birdies: ___
Pars: ___   Sand saves: ___/___
Bogeys: ___
DB+:   ___   Putts: ___

F.I.R.:   /

L Trouble	L Rough	Fairway	R Rough	R Trouble

G.I.R.:   / 18

Key area(s) to improve:

_____

_____

Weekly practice: technique

Practice aims:

1. _____

2. _____

Technical thoughts:

Desired change in ball flight:

Key pieces of feedback:

Summary

Number of reps completed: _____

Percentage of good swings: _____

Areas to improve in practice:

_____

_____

_____

Weekly practice: skills games

Skill game 1: *Hugo's range challenge*

Set up & notes:

Difficulty:

Score:

Time/reps completed:

_____

Skill game 2: *Putting drill basics*

Set up & notes:

Difficulty:

Score: /20

Time/reps completed:

_____

Skill game 3:

Set up & notes:

Difficulty:

Score:

Time/reps completed:

Weekly notes:

Weekly playing stats

Score to par: ___   Net score: ___

Eagles: ___   Up & downs: ___/___
Birdies: ___
Pars: ___   Sand saves: ___/___
Bogeys: ___
DB+:   ___   Putts: ___

F.I.R.:   /

L Trouble	L Rough	Fairway	R Rough	R Trouble

G.I.R.:   / 18

Key area(s) to improve:

_____

_____

Weekly practice: technique

Practice aims:

1. _____

2. _____

Technical thoughts:

Desired change in ball flight:

Key pieces of feedback:

Summary

Number of reps completed: _____

Percentage of good swings: _____

Areas to improve in practice:

_____

_____

_____

Weekly practice: skills games

Skill game 1: *Hugo's range challenge*

Set up & notes:

Difficulty:

Score:

Time/reps completed:

Skill game 2: *Putting drill basics*

Set up & notes:

Difficulty:

Score:

Time/reps completed:

Skill game 3:

Set up & notes:

Difficulty:

Score:

Time/reps completed:

Weekly notes:

Week 5: Chipping zone

This week we are going to cement one last skills game into your schedule. After this week I will let you choose which skills games you use each week.

However, I hope these first few weeks have given you a feel for how you can build your own weekly practice schedule.

Think back over your *up and down* stats. What are the types of chip shots that you would like to improve? It may be a high, short chip, or a longer chip and run. Pick a chip shot that you frequently require when you play.

Set a distance and type of shot, then play the following game to begin improving your chipping skill.

Hover your phone camera over the QR code to see a video version (the set up is slightly easier in this version), or follow the instructions below.

http://golfinsideruk.com/golf-chipping-practice-lower-your-scores/

On a chipping green set up the following:

Pick a hole and make a circle of tees around the hole at one 9 Iron length. Create a second ring of tees another 9 Iron length away. This should create one small circle (3ft) and one big circle (6ft), with your target in the centre.

You score points as follows:

In the hole = 4 points
Small circle = 2 points
Big circle = 1 point

The game – you have 10 shots from your chosen location to see how many points you can score. Add up your points after your 10 shots and write down your total. This is your score.

When you've hit all 10 shots, take a note of your shot distribution. Are your chip shots finishing short/long, or to one side? Use this information to refine your technique and decision making on your next attempt.

You can play this can two, three or four times in a row to see if you can beat your previous top score. This is a great way to improve your chipping.

Weekly playing stats

Score to par: ___   Net score: ___

Eagles: ___   Up & downs: ___/___
Birdies: ___
Pars: ___   Sand saves: ___/___
Bogeys: ___
DB+:   ___   Putts: ___

F.I.R.:   /

L Trouble	L Rough	Fairway	R Rough	R Trouble

G.I.R.:   / 18

Key area(s) to improve:

_____

_____

Weekly practice: technique

Practice aims:

1. _____

2. _____

Technical thoughts:

Desired change in ball flight:

Key pieces of feedback:

Summary

Number of reps completed: _____

Percentage of good swings: _____

Areas to improve in practice:

_____

_____

_____

Weekly practice: skills games

Skill game 1: *Hugo's range challenge*

Set up & notes:

Difficulty:

Score:

Time/reps completed:

_____

Skill game 2: *Putting drill basics*

Set up & notes:

Difficulty:

Score:

Time/reps completed:

_____

Skill game 3: *Chipping zone challenge*

Set up & notes:

Difficulty:

Score:

Time/reps completed:

Weekly notes:

Completed Week Five

Congratulations, you're flying! If you have consistently stuck to the plan to this point, you'll be ready for your golfing rewards.

Don't worry if your investment hasn't started to feed into your play just yet. From my experience, it takes two to eight weeks for the results to really shine through.

I'd love to see how you're getting on. Please take a pic of your favourite page, or your 'ruffled' performance diary on your home golf course.

You can send me a picture at @golfinsideruk on Twitter or Instagram.

Weekly playing stats

Score to par: ___   Net score: ___

Eagles: ___   Up & downs: ___/___
Birdies: ___
Pars: ___   Sand saves: ___/___
Bogeys: ___
DB+:   ___   Putts: ___

F.I.R.:   /

L Trouble	L Rough	Fairway	R Rough	R Trouble

G.I.R.:   / 18

Key area(s) to improve:

_____

_____

Weekly practice: technique

Practice aims:

1. _____

2. _____

Technical thoughts:

Desired change in ball flight:

Key pieces of feedback:

Summary

Number of reps completed: _____

Percentage of good swings: _____

Areas to improve in practice:

_____

_____

_____

Weekly practice: skills games

Skill game 1: *Hugo's range challenge*

Set up & notes:

Difficulty:

Score:

Time/reps completed:

_____

Skill game 2: *Putting drill basics*

Set up & notes:

Difficulty:

Score:

Time/reps completed:

_____

Skill game 3: *Chipping zone challenge*

Set up & notes:

Difficulty:

Score:

Time/reps completed:

Weekly notes:

Week 7: Wedge challenge

This week we are going to take your practice onto the golf course. I understand that not all of you may be able to play this around your home golf course and play it exactly as I describe it. However, do your best to adapt it to fit your surroundings.

The game is called wedge challenge, it can be played over 9 holes on its own, or whilst you knock another ball round one evening.

Nine holes golf, and on each hole you hit a ball in from 125, 100 and 75 yards. Your aim/score is to see how many pars or birdies you can make.

Easy/Medium: 1 point for every Par

Hard/Pro: 1 point for every Birdie

If you score worse than your target score, don't worry, just pick up and move on.

This game is great for transferring your golfing skill onto the course. You will see common trends in shot direction, and realise how tough it actually is to hit your wedges close.

The realistic nature of this game will really help your play. Try it this week, and then aim to play it once per month to keep your wedge game sharp.

Weekly playing stats

Score to par: ___   Net score: ___

Eagles: ___   Up & downs: ___/___
Birdies: ___
Pars: ___   Sand saves: ___/___
Bogeys: ___
DB+:   ___   Putts: ___

F.I.R.:   /

L Trouble	L Rough	Fairway	R Rough	R Trouble

G.I.R.:   / 18

Key area(s) to improve:

_____

_____

Weekly practice: technique

Practice aims:

1. _____

2. _____

Technical thoughts:

Desired change in ball flight:

Key pieces of feedback:

Summary

Number of reps completed: _____

Percentage of good swings: _____

Areas to improve in practice:

_____

_____

_____

Weekly practice: skills games

Skill game 1: *Wedge challenge*

Set up & notes:

Difficulty:

Score:

Time/reps completed:

Skill game 2:

Set up & notes:

Difficulty:

Score:

Time/reps completed:

Skill game 3:

Set up & notes:

Difficulty:

Score:

Time/reps completed:

Weekly notes:

Weekly playing stats

Score to par: ___   Net score: ___

Eagles: ___   Up & downs: ___/___
Birdies: ___
Pars: ___   Sand saves: ___/___
Bogeys: ___
DB+:   ___   Putts: ___

F.I.R.:   /

L Trouble	L Rough	Fairway	R Rough	R Trouble

G.I.R.:   / 18

Key area(s) to improve:

_____

_____

Weekly practice: technique

Practice aims:

1. _____

2. _____

Technical thoughts:

Desired change in ball flight:

Key pieces of feedback:

Summary

Number of reps completed: _____

Percentage of good swings: _____

Areas to improve in practice:

_____

_____

_____

Weekly practice: skills games

Skill game 1:

Set up & notes:

Difficulty:

Score:

Time/reps completed:

Skill game 2:

Set up & notes:

Difficulty:

Score:

Time/reps completed:

Skill game 3:

Set up & notes:

Difficulty:

Score:

Time/reps completed:

Weekly notes:

Week 9: Will's range challenge

The next game I would like you to try is my very own range challenge. I built this, played it and have gifted it to many golfers.

It aims to add consequence and variability to your range practice. To play it, you will need to head to your golf range/practice ground and grab 50 balls. You have six stages to complete and you must complete each stage before you can move onto the next.

If you want a re-cap on long game skills games and their purpose check out the QR code or the link below.

http://golfinsideruk.com/golf-practice-games-long-game/

Then follow these instructions:

Set up: Create a 20-yard fairway on your range using two targets. Then find/create or imagine small greens (approx. 10 yard diameter) at 100, 150 and 200 yards.

Aim to complete the following stages in order:

1. Hit two drivers in a row that land in your fairway.

2. Hit two shots with a fairway wood that land in your fairway.

3. Hit two shots with a long iron that land in your fairway.

4. Hit two shots in a row that land on your 100 yards green.

5. Hit two shots in a row that land on your 150 yards green.

6. Hit two shots in a row that land on your 200 yards green.

Your aim is to see what stage you can get to with your 50 balls, but if you are struggling, start off with one ball to complete each stage. To make it harder, advance to three balls for each stage.

For the pros I work with, we remove the greens and I ask them to hit the 100/150/200 yard sign or flag stick.

This may sound crazy, but you have to make sure the difficulty of your practice keeps moving forward in line with your golfing skill.

You don't have to complete this game, but enjoy the challenge it gives you.

Weekly playing stats

Score to par: ___   Net score: ___

Eagles: ___   Up & downs: ___/___
Birdies: ___
Pars: ___   Sand saves: ___/___
Bogeys: ___
DB+:   ___   Putts: ___

F.I.R.:   /

L Trouble	L Rough	Fairway	R Rough	R Trouble

G.I.R.:   / 18

Key area(s) to improve:

_____

_____

Weekly practice: technique

Practice aims:

1. _____

2. _____

Technical thoughts:

Desired change in ball flight:

Key pieces of feedback:

Summary

Number of reps completed: _____

Percentage of good swings: _____

Areas to improve in practice:

_____

_____

_____

Weekly practice: skills games

Skill game 1: *Will's range challenge*

Set up & notes:

Difficulty:

Score:

Time/reps completed:

_____

Skill game 2:

Set up & notes:

Difficulty:

Score:

Time/reps completed:

_____

Skill game 3:

Set up & notes:

Difficulty:

Score:

Time/reps completed:

Weekly notes:

Weekly playing stats

Score to par: ___   Net score: ___

Eagles: ___   Up & downs: ___/___
Birdies: ___
Pars: ___   Sand saves: ___/___
Bogeys: ___
DB+:   ___   Putts: ___

F.I.R.:   /

L Trouble	L Rough	Fairway	R Rough	R Trouble

G.I.R.:   / 18

Key area(s) to improve:

_____

_____

Weekly practice: technique

Practice aims:

1. _____

2. _____

Technical thoughts:

Desired change in ball flight:

Key pieces of feedback:

Summary

Number of reps completed: _____

Percentage of good swings: _____

Areas to improve in practice:

_____

_____

_____

Weekly practice: skills games

Skill game 1: *Will's range challenge*

Set up & notes:

Difficulty:

Score:

Time/reps completed:

_____

Skill game 2:

Set up & notes:

Difficulty:

Score:

Time/reps completed:

_____

Skill game 3:

Set up & notes:

Difficulty:

Score:

Time/reps completed:

Weekly notes:

Week 11: Golf technique 1

For this week's task there is a shift in focus. I hope you've enjoyed the barrage of new practice ideas we've covered to date.

I've front-loaded this edition with these skills games, as they are missing from many golfers' practice and are critical in developing your golfing skill.

Now I want you to reflect on your technical ability. Look back through your playing stats. Where do you miss your tee shots and approach shots? What patterns have emerged?

I want you to take one of these misses and take time to improve this area with your golf coach. If you don't have a great golf coach, I urge you to find one.

Whether you have a coach or not, I feel it is important that you understand the basics of golf coaching and ball flight. This will help you to manage your technique and play well.

http://golfinsideruk.com/how-to-be-your-own-golf-coach/

Read the article above, then the next time you are at the golf range answer the questions below. Note: this list may not make sense until you have read the article.

1. What is the desired shot shape I want to hit more often?

2. What changes as the golf club hits the ball to cause your good and bad shots?

3. What swing principles do I need to focus on to improve my impact?

4. How do I know I have made the correct movements? (Think about how you are gaining feedback).

5. Can I over-exaggerate a movement to get the opposite shot shape?

Being able to answer these questions ensures you have the knowledge to improve your technique and golf performance.

It also summarises the basics of golf coaching that we, as pros, use to build and develop your golf swing.

Weekly playing stats

Score to par: ___   Net score: ___

Eagles: ___   Up & downs: ___/___
Birdies: ___
Pars: ___   Sand saves: ___/___
Bogeys: ___
DB+:   ___   Putts: ___

F.I.R.:   /

L Trouble	L Rough	Fairway	R Rough	R Trouble

G.I.R.:   / 18

Key area(s) to improve:

_____

_____

Weekly practice: technique

Practice aims:

1. _____

2. _____

Technical thoughts:

Desired change in ball flight:

Key pieces of feedback:

Summary

Number of reps completed: _____

Percentage of good swings: _____

Areas to improve in practice:

_____

_____

_____

Weekly practice: skills games

Skill game 1:

Set up & notes:

Difficulty:

Score:

Time/reps completed:

Skill game 2:

Set up & notes:

Difficulty:

Score:

Time/reps completed:

Skill game 3:

Set up & notes:

Difficulty:

Score:

Time/reps completed:

Weekly notes:

Weekly playing stats

Score to par: ___   Net score: ___

Eagles: ___   Up & downs: ___/___
Birdies: ___
Pars: ___   Sand saves: ___/___
Bogeys: ___
DB+:   ___   Putts: ___

F.I.R.:   /

L Trouble	L Rough	Fairway	R Rough	R Trouble

G.I.R.:   / 18

Key area(s) to improve:

_____

_____

Weekly practice: technique

Practice aims:

1. _____

2. _____

Technical thoughts:

Desired change in ball flight:

Key pieces of feedback:

Summary

Number of reps completed: _____

Percentage of good swings: _____

Areas to improve in practice:

_____

_____

_____

Weekly practice: skills games

Skill game 1:

Set up & notes:

Difficulty:

Score:

Time/reps completed:

_____

Skill game 2:

Set up & notes:

Difficulty:

Score:

Time/reps completed:

_____

Skill game 3:

Set up & notes:

Difficulty:

Score:

Time/reps completed:

Weekly notes:

Week 13: Golf technique 2

This week we cover the second part of how to improve your technique. We covered the following article many weeks ago, but please use the links below to re-read the technique section on 3 ways to practice.

http://golfinsideruk.com/golf-practice-3-ways-practice-golf/

The aim of this week is to really consider how you should structure your technique practice. In the article I outline six steps to take you from making a technical change, to taking this change in technique onto the golf course. As you move from stages 1 to 6 you will find it progressively harder to correctly replicate your swing changes.

This is actually a good thing, when you make mistakes, your body is forced to adapt and learn. In your future weeks of technical practice try to mix up your practice structure. When you start hitting 8 out of 10 shots well, move onto the next stage of practice. This will continually force your body to *learn* the desired technique.

Weekly playing stats

Score to par: ____   Net score: ____

Eagles: ____   Up & downs: ___/___
Birdies: ____
Pars: ____   Sand saves: ___/___
Bogeys: ____
DB+:   ____   Putts: ___

F.I.R.:   /

L Trouble	L Rough	Fairway	R Rough	R Trouble

G.I.R.:   / 18

Key area(s) to improve:

_____

_____

Weekly practice: technique

Practice aims:

1. _____

2. _____

Technical thoughts:

Desired change in ball flight:

Key pieces of feedback:

Summary

Number of reps completed: _____

Percentage of good swings: _____

Areas to improve in practice:

_____

_____

_____

Weekly practice: skills games

Skill game 1:

Set up & notes:

Difficulty:

Score:

Time/reps completed:

_____

Skill game 2:

Set up & notes:

Difficulty:

Score:

Time/reps completed:

_____

Skill game 3:

Set up & notes:

Difficulty:

Score:

Time/reps completed:

Weekly notes:

Weekly playing stats

Score to par: ___   Net score: ___

Eagles: ___   Up & downs: ___/___
Birdies: ___
Pars: ___   Sand saves: ___/___
Bogeys: ___
DB+:   ___   Putts: ___

F.I.R.:   /

L Trouble	L Rough	Fairway	R Rough	R Trouble

G.I.R.:   / 18

Key area(s) to improve:

_____

_____

Weekly practice: technique

Practice aims:

1. _____

2. _____

Technical thoughts:

Desired change in ball flight:

Key pieces of feedback:

Summary

Number of reps completed: _____

Percentage of good swings: _____

Areas to improve in practice:

_____

_____

_____

Weekly practice: skills games

Skill game 1:

Set up & notes:

Difficulty:

Score:

Time/reps completed:

Skill game 2:

Set up & notes:

Difficulty:

Score:

Time/reps completed:

Skill game 3:

Set up & notes:

Difficulty:

Score:

Time/reps completed:

Weekly notes:

Week 15: Par 18

This week I want to get back to some great ways to improve your short game and scoring. Check out the following article with three chipping skills games.

http://golfinsideruk.com/golf-chipping-practice-lower-your-scores/

Feel free to try all of them, but the one I want you to focus on is Par 18. It really is one of my all-time favourite practice games.

Around your chipping green (or whilst the golf course is quiet) grab one club to chip with and your putter.

Set up: Choose 9 locations to chip from. Try to pick 3 easy, 3 medium and 3 hard chip shots. Your aim is to chip from each location, and hole out the putt. This would give you a score of 2. It is medal play; so keep your score for each hole.

If you get up and down for all 9 shots you will achieve the par of 18 – hence the name.

Weekly playing stats

Score to par: ___   Net score: ___

Eagles: ___   Up & downs: ___/___
Birdies: ___
Pars: ___   Sand saves: ___/___
Bogeys: ___
DB+:   ___   Putts: ___

F.I.R.:   /

L Trouble	L Rough	Fairway	R Rough	R Trouble

G.I.R.:   / 18

Key area(s) to improve:

_____

_____

Weekly practice: technique

Practice aims:

1. _____

2. _____

Technical thoughts:

Desired change in ball flight:

Key pieces of feedback:

Summary

Number of reps completed: _____

Percentage of good swings: _____

Areas to improve in practice:

_____

_____

_____

Weekly practice: skills games

Skill game 1: *Par 18*

Set up & notes:

Difficulty:

Score:

Time/reps completed:

Skill game 2:

Set up & notes:

Difficulty:

Score:

Time/reps completed:

Skill game 3:

Set up & notes:

Difficulty:

Score:

Time/reps completed:

Weekly notes:

Weekly playing stats

Score to par: ___   Net score: ___

Eagles: ___   Up & downs: ___/___
Birdies: ___
Pars: ___   Sand saves: ___/___
Bogeys: ___
DB+:   ___   Putts: ___

F.I.R.:   /

L Trouble	L Rough	Fairway	R Rough	R Trouble

G.I.R.:   / 18

Key area(s) to improve:

_____

_____

Weekly practice: technique

Practice aims:

1. _____

2. _____

Technical thoughts:

Desired change in ball flight:

Key pieces of feedback:

Summary

Number of reps completed: _____

Percentage of good swings: _____

Areas to improve in practice:

_____

_____

_____

Weekly practice: skills games

Skill game 1: *Par 18*

Set up & notes:

Difficulty:

Score:

Time/reps completed:

_____

Skill game 2:

Set up & notes:

Difficulty:

Score:

Time/reps completed:

_____

Skill game 3:

Set up & notes:

Difficulty:

Score:

Time/reps completed:

Weekly notes:

Week 17: No G.I.R.

We've covered a lot of ground so far on this journey. I hope your golf is making fine progress, and that you're having fun with these new practices.

This week I would like to introduce two new skills games that involve the golf course. The golf range allows you to hit many shots in a short period of time. However, it does not match the environment you will be playing competitively in. For this reason it is also important to practice on the golf course.

The following games can be played over 9 or 18 holes.

In Regulation: This is a very simple game where you gain points for hitting fairways and greens in regulation. Give yourself 1 point for every fairway you hit and 2 points for every green you hit in regulation. Focus on scoring points, not the number of strokes it takes you to complete each hole.

No G.I.R.: Only play this game if you are a serious golfer, or you love pain. Your aim is to shoot the best medal score you can without hitting a green in regulation. If you hit a green in regulation your playing partner gets to throw your ball off in any chosen direction.

This second game takes golf to a whole new level of difficulty. Enjoy.

Weekly playing stats

Score to par: ___   Net score: ___

Eagles: ___   Up & downs: ___/___
Birdies: ___
Pars: ___   Sand saves: ___/___
Bogeys: ___
DB+:   ___   Putts: ___

F.I.R.:   /

L Trouble	L Rough	Fairway	R Rough	R Trouble

G.I.R.:   / 18

Key area(s) to improve:

_____

_____

Weekly practice: technique

Practice aims:

1. _____

2. _____

Technical thoughts:

Desired change in ball flight:

Key pieces of feedback:

Summary

Number of reps completed: _____

Percentage of good swings: _____

Areas to improve in practice:

_____

_____

_____

Weekly practice: skills games

Skill game 1: *No GIR (I dare you)*

Set up & notes:

Difficulty:

Score:

Time/reps completed:

_____

Skill game 2:

Set up & notes:

Difficulty:

Score:

Time/reps completed:

_____

Skill game 3:

Set up & notes:

Difficulty:

Score:

Time/reps completed:

Weekly notes:

Weekly playing stats

Score to par: ___   Net score: ___

Eagles: ___   Up & downs: ___/___
Birdies: ___
Pars: ___   Sand saves: ___/___
Bogeys: ___
DB+:   ___   Putts: ___

F.I.R.:   /

L Trouble	L Rough	Fairway	R Rough	R Trouble

G.I.R.:   / 18

Key area(s) to improve:

_____

_____

Weekly practice: technique

Practice aims:

1. _____

2. _____

Technical thoughts:

Desired change in ball flight:

Key pieces of feedback:

Summary

Number of reps completed: _____

Percentage of good swings: _____

Areas to improve in practice:

_____

_____

_____

Weekly practice: skills games

Skill game 1:

Set up & notes:

Difficulty:

Score:

Time/reps completed:

_____

Skill game 2:

Set up & notes:

Difficulty:

Score:

Time/reps completed:

_____

Skill game 3:

Set up & notes:

Difficulty:

Score:

Time/reps completed:

Weekly notes:

Week 19: Practice difficulty

As we move towards the end of this journey I want to make sure you're not only a better golfer, but also have more knowledge about how to practice and improve.

This week I would like you to revisit your favourite skills games and work out how you can adapt these games to keep them suitably challenging. To help you, I have included the following article.

http://golfinsideruk.com/golf-practice-difficult/

Think specifically about what you want to make more challenging. If I think back to your first putting skills challenge (week 3) I have three simple ways I could make it more difficult:

- Increase the distance of each putt.
- Reduce the target size.
- Vary the distance between repetitions.

Create some new adaptations of your favourite games and try them out over the following two weeks.

Weekly playing stats

Score to par: ___   Net score: ___

Eagles: ___   Up & downs: ___/___
Birdies: ___
Pars: ___   Sand saves: ___/___
Bogeys: ___
DB+:   ___   Putts: ___

F.I.R.:   /

L Trouble	L Rough	Fairway	R Rough	R Trouble

G.I.R.:   / 18

Key area(s) to improve:

_____

_____

Weekly practice: technique

Practice aims:

1. _____

2. _____

Technical thoughts:

Desired change in ball flight:

Key pieces of feedback:

Summary

Number of reps completed: _____

Percentage of good swings: _____

Areas to improve in practice:

_____

_____

_____

Weekly practice: skills games

Skill game 1:

Set up & notes:

Difficulty:

Score:

Time/reps completed:

Skill game 2:

Set up & notes:

Difficulty:

Score:

Time/reps completed:

Skill game 3:

Set up & notes:

Difficulty:

Score:

Time/reps completed:

Weekly notes:

Weekly playing stats

Score to par: ____   Net score: ____

Eagles: ____   Up & downs: ___/___
Birdies: ____
Pars: ____   Sand saves: ___/___
Bogeys: ____
DB+:   ____   Putts: ____

F.I.R.:   /

L Trouble	L Rough	Fairway	R Rough	R Trouble

G.I.R.:   / 18

Key area(s) to improve:

_____

_____

Weekly practice: technique

Practice aims:

1. _____

2. _____

Technical thoughts:

Desired change in ball flight:

Key pieces of feedback:

Summary

Number of reps completed: _____

Percentage of good swings: _____

Areas to improve in practice:

_____

_____

_____

Weekly practice: skills games

Skill game 1:

Set up & notes:

Difficulty:

Score:

Time/reps completed:

Skill game 2:

Set up & notes:

Difficulty:

Score:

Time/reps completed:

Skill game 3:

Set up & notes:

Difficulty:

Score:

Time/reps completed:

Weekly notes:

Week 21: Over to you

For now I am about to say goodbye. I hope that you have found this performance diary useful in developing your golfing skill and knowledge.

It is now over to you to take charge of the following few weeks. Reflect on your playing stats and keep finding the areas that are holding you back from lower scores.

For next week, I would like you to pick three skills games that focus on areas you need to improve most. Include these games in next week's practice. If you need some fresh ideas, subscribe to the golf insider weekly post or send me an email.

http://golfinsideruk.com/golf-insiders/

I'd love to hear how your golf has progressed – find me on Twitter or Instagram @golfinsideruk.

All the best and happy golfing!

Will.

Weekly playing stats

Score to par: ____   Net score: ____

Eagles: ____   Up & downs: ___/___
Birdies: ____
Pars: ____   Sand saves: ___/___
Bogeys: ____
DB+:   ____   Putts: ____

F.I.R.:   /

L Trouble	L Rough	Fairway	R Rough	R Trouble

G.I.R.:   / 18

Key area(s) to improve:

_____

_____

Weekly practice: technique

Practice aims:

1. _____

2. _____

Technical thoughts:

Desired change in ball flight:

Key pieces of feedback:

Summary

Number of reps completed: _____

Percentage of good swings: _____

Areas to improve in practice:

_____

_____

_____

Weekly practice: skills games

Skill game 1:

Set up & notes:

Difficulty:

Score:

Time/reps completed:

_____

Skill game 2:

Set up & notes:

Difficulty:

Score:

Time/reps completed:

_____

Skill game 3:

Set up & notes:

Difficulty:

Score:

Time/reps completed:

Weekly notes:

Weekly playing stats

Score to par: ___   Net score: ___

Eagles: ___   Up & downs: ___/___
Birdies: ___
Pars: ___   Sand saves: ___/___
Bogeys: ___
DB+:   ___   Putts: ___

F.I.R.:   /

L Trouble	L Rough	Fairway	R Rough	R Trouble

G.I.R.:   / 18

Key area(s) to improve:

_____

_____

Weekly practice: technique

Practice aims:

1. _____

2. _____

Technical thoughts:

Desired change in ball flight:

Key pieces of feedback:

Summary

Number of reps completed: _____

Percentage of good swings: _____

Areas to improve in practice:

_____

_____

_____

Weekly practice: skills games

Skill game 1:

Set up & notes:

Difficulty:

Score:

Time/reps completed:

Skill game 2:

Set up & notes:

Difficulty:

Score:

Time/reps completed:

Skill game 3:

Set up & notes:

Difficulty:

Score:

Time/reps completed:

Weekly notes:

Weekly playing stats

Score to par: ___   Net score: ___

Eagles: ___   Up & downs: ___/___
Birdies: ___
Pars: ___   Sand saves: ___/___
Bogeys: ___
DB+:   ___   Putts: ___

F.I.R.:   /

L Trouble	L Rough	Fairway	R Rough	R Trouble

G.I.R.:   / 18

Key area(s) to improve:

_____

_____

Weekly practice: technique

Practice aims:

1. _____

2. _____

Technical thoughts:

Desired change in ball flight:

Key pieces of feedback:

Summary

Number of reps completed: _____

Percentage of good swings: _____

Areas to improve in practice:

_____

_____

_____

Weekly practice: skills games

Skill game 1:

Set up & notes:

Difficulty:

Score:

Time/reps completed:

Skill game 2:

Set up & notes:

Difficulty:

Score:

Time/reps completed:

Skill game 3:

Set up & notes:

Difficulty:

Score:

Time/reps completed:

Weekly notes:

Weekly playing stats

Score to par: ___   Net score: ___

Eagles: ___   Up & downs: ___/___
Birdies: ___
Pars: ___   Sand saves: ___/___
Bogeys: ___
DB+:   ___   Putts: ___

F.I.R.:   /

L Trouble	L Rough	Fairway	R Rough	R Trouble

G.I.R.:   / 18

Key area(s) to improve:

_____

_____

Weekly practice: technique

Practice aims:

1. _____

2. _____

Technical thoughts:

Desired change in ball flight:

Key pieces of feedback:

Summary

Number of reps completed: _____

Percentage of good swings: _____

Areas to improve in practice:

_____

_____

_____

Weekly practice: skills games

Skill game 1:

Set up & notes:

Difficulty:

Score:

Time/reps completed:

Skill game 2:

Set up & notes:

Difficulty:

Score:

Time/reps completed:

Skill game 3:

Set up & notes:

Difficulty:

Score:

Time/reps completed:

Weekly notes:

Weekly playing stats

Score to par: ___   Net score: ___

Eagles: ___   Up & downs: ___/___
Birdies: ___
Pars: ___   Sand saves: ___/___
Bogeys: ___
DB+:   ___   Putts: ___

F.I.R.:   /

L Trouble	L Rough	Fairway	R Rough	R Trouble

G.I.R.:   / 18

Key area(s) to improve:

_____

_____

Weekly practice: technique

Practice aims:

1. _____

2. _____

Technical thoughts:

Desired change in ball flight:

Key pieces of feedback:

Summary

Number of reps completed: _____

Percentage of good swings: _____

Areas to improve in practice:

_____

_____

_____

Weekly practice: skills games

Skill game 1:

Set up & notes:

Difficulty:

Score:

Time/reps completed:

_____

Skill game 2:

Set up & notes:

Difficulty:

Score:

Time/reps completed:

_____

Skill game 3:

Set up & notes:

Difficulty:

Score:

Time/reps completed:

Weekly notes:

Printed in Great Britain
by Amazon

24578116R00078